CHOO CHOO
clickety-clack!

**For Natalie, Madeleine
and Eòin
MM**

**For Jay and Danny
AA**

ORCHARD BOOKS

First published in Great Britain in 2004
by Orchard Books
This edition first published in 2016

03 05 07 09 10 08 06 04 02

Text © Margaret Mayo 2004
Illustrations © Alex Ayliffe 2004

The moral rights of the author
and illustrator have been asserted.

A CIP catalogue record for this book
is available from the British Library.

ISBN 978 1 40834 928 1

Printed and bound in China

Orchard Books
An imprint of Hachette Children's Group
Part of The Watts Publishing Group Limited
Carmelite House, 50 Victoria Embankment, London EC4Y 0DZ

An Hachette UK Company
www.hachette.co.uk
www.hachettechildrens.co.uk

CHOO CHOO
Clickety-clack!

written by **Margaret Mayo**   illustrated by **Alex Ayliffe**

ORCHARD

Trains are great at speed, speed, **speeding,**
Tooting - whooo-hooo!
Through tunnels rattling, at stations stopping;
Choo choo, clickety-clack! **Off they go!**

Aeroplanes are great at fly, fly, flying,
To faraway places people carrying,
Zooming down runways – up, up and away – soaring;
WhoarrrRR! Off they go!

Cars are great at drive, drive, **driving**,
To shops, to friends or a special outing,
Quick packing, seats choosing, belts fastening;
Beep-beep! Off they go!

Racing cars are great at race, race, **racing**,
waiting at the starting line, crouching, growling,
Hurtling round the track, chase, chase, chasing;
Grrumm, grrumm! Off they go!

Sailing boats are great at sail, sail, sailing,
Over waves bouncing,
Water slap-slapping, sails flapping;
Flappety-flap! Off they go!

Hot-air balloons are great at float, float, floating,

High in the sky glide, gliding.

Filling, swelling and rising;

Whoo-oosh! Off they go!

Motorbikes are great at roar, roar, roaring,

Swooping, swerving and overtaking.

Careful now – no crashing!

Vroom, vroom! Off they go!

Cycles are great at whiz, whiz, **whizzing**,

They have no engines, just pedals for pushing,

But they shoot by, wheels whirl, whirling;
Zippety-zip! Off they go!

Cable cars are great at climb, climb, climbing,
Up the mountain swiftly swinging.
Hurry in, skiers – doors closing;
Shlum
p! Whurr-rr! Off they go!

Buses are great at travel, travel, **travelling**,
Always at the same time, the same route following,
Ding-ding! Always stopping and starting;
Brumm, brumm! Off they go!

Ferryboats are great at load, load, **loading,**
Cars and trucks parking, people boarding.

Ready to leave! **Pomp, pomp,** hooter sounding;
Chug, chug! Off they go!

Now it is dark – many vehicles are resting,
But some keep travelling just as fast,
Still zoom-zooming and clickety-clacking;
On they go till they are **home at last!**

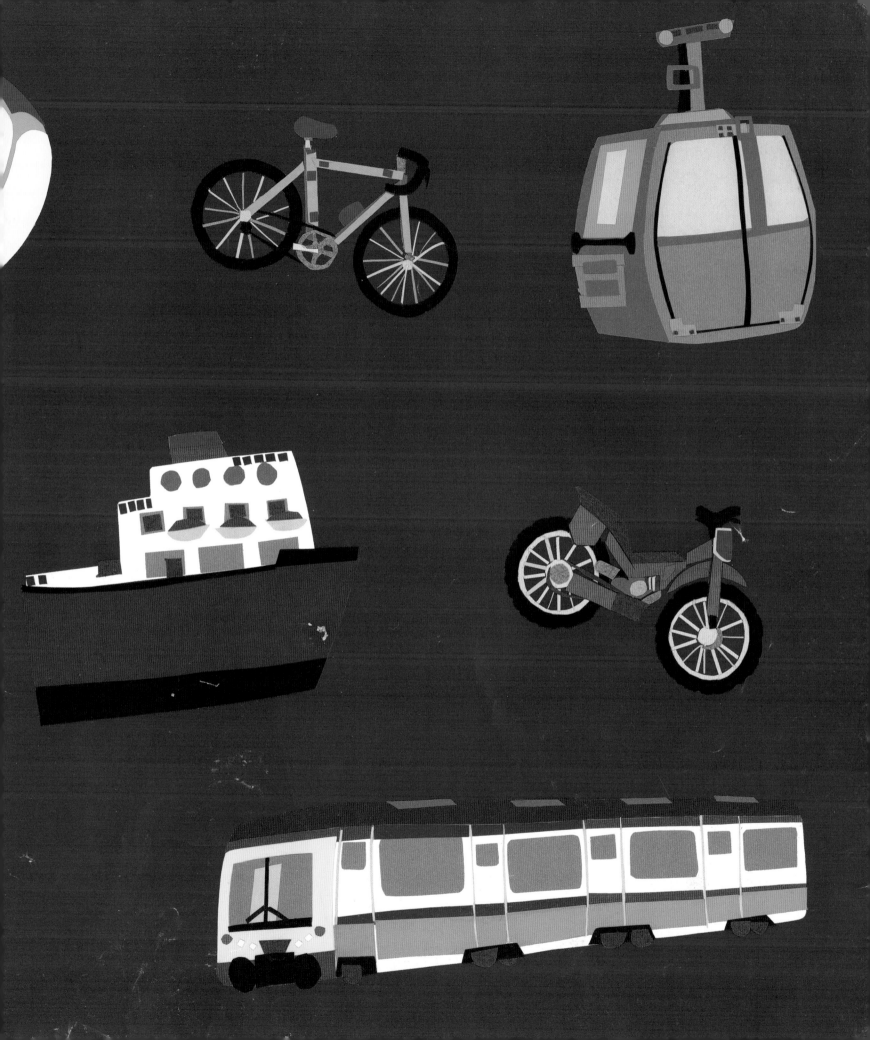